DOUGLAS DC-3

Kengo Yamamoto

DOUGLAS DC-3
THE SURVIVORS

Airlife

England

First published in the UK in 2000
by Airlife Publishing Ltd

British Library Cataloguing-in-Publication Data
 A catalogue record for this book
 is available from the British Library

ISBN 1 84037 152 8

The information in this book is true and complete to the best of our
knowledge. All recommendations are made without any guarantee on the
part of the Publisher, who also disclaims any liability incurred in
connection with the use of this data or specific details.

Printed in Hong Kong

Airlife Publishing Ltd
101 Longden Road, Shrewsbury, SY3 9EB, England
E-mail: airlife@airlifebooks.com
Website: www.airlifebooks.com

CONTENTS

INTRODUCTION

This is an illustrated guide to many of the remaining Douglas DC-3 family of aircraft. They have been photographed in a variety of museums, airfields and during restoration. Aircraft are identified and wherever possible a brief history of the aircraft is supplied.

DC-3 FAMILIES

Originally one of Eastern Airlines' ten DC-2-112s, and acquired by the RAAF in March 1941, this aircraft is preserved at Albury airport, NSW. Painted in the colours of KLM it celebrates the incident when PH-AJU *Uiver* (Stork), a DC-2, c/n 1317, made an emergency landing at Albury during the London to Melbourne MacRobertson Trophy Race on 24 October 1934, about 160 miles short of its 11,123 mile goal. It flew on to gain second place in a time of 90 hours 17 minutes. *Uiver* later crashed at Rutbah Wells, Iraq on 20 December 1934. Forty-four, painted on the fin and under the nose, is its racing number. Control surfaces were replaced in metal for the display. (Photo September 1996)

Restoration of A30-9, a DC-2-112, was begun in October 1982 at Essendon Airport, Victoria and completed in November 1984 by Jack McDonald and Tim Wright. Some years later she was taken to Western Port Airfield at Tyabb, Victoria where most parts – wings, engines, fuel tanks, rudder, elevators, floor and seats – were removed and are now hangared by the owner, Jack McDonald of the Tyabb Airport Collection. Note the fixed nose landing light, the narrow vertical stabiliser and lack of wing fillet. A30 was the code for RAAF DC-2s and A65 for C-47s. (Photo November 1996)

This DC-2-115G, VH-CDZ, is under restoration at the Qantas training school, Alexandria, NSW. Most parts have been removed for restoration. The front windscreen is in a custom-made frame, the original DC-2 window consisting of two pieces of glass joined by a rubber strip. (Photo December 1996)

There are nine surviving DC-2s in the world with only two in flyable condition. Hopefully, in the near future, a third will be restored to flyable standard in Australia and in about fifteen years the Dutch Dakota Association will have the fourth, if their project goes ahead. This DC-2-118B, N1934D, at the Douglas Historical Foundation, Long Beach, CA, USA has the Wright engine and an early cowling with a DC-3 oil-cooler air-scoop. The fin is from a later-model DC-2. Note the large Douglas sign on the upper wing. Since the merger of Douglas and Boeing the aircraft will be displayed at air shows and used for PR purposes. (Photo January 1997)

This DC-2-243/C-39 in early USAAF colours is in the collection hangar of the United States Air Force Museum, Wright-Patterson AFB, Dayton, OH. The museum has the largest collection of aircraft in the world, with many aircraft loaned to Air Force museums and bases. They have thirty-eight DC-3s and one DC-2. The C-39 has DC-3 landing gear, centre section and tail, and has 975 hp Wright engines. It was sometimes known as the DC-2½. Thirty-five were built with a cargo door. This C-39 is the last surviving example of the type. (Photo September 1997)

The Super 3 had its maiden flight at Clover Field on 23 June 1949. Douglas converted a total of 105 aircraft, 5 for civil use as DC-3Ss, and 100 as R4D-8s for navy use. After World War II Douglas tried to convert the many surplus C-47s to modern systems and higher-power engines, but civil sales were poor. This aircraft, N30000, in Tucson, AZ, is the first R4D-8 in Super 3 demonstration colour scheme and register, used by Douglas for a US sales tour. Despite its good capacity, Super 3 sales suffered due to its expense. The fuselage was lengthened by 3 feet 3 inches and extra windows installed. Note the one-piece windscreen, the nose intake, new engine nacelles and undercarriage doors, shorter, trailing wings, flush rivets on the centre panel and wing, large dorsal fin for increased engine power, retractable tail wheel and new tail unit. The engines are Wright Cyclone R-1820 (1475 hp) nine-cylinder radials. (Photo February 1997)

This aircraft was built as a C-47B-20-DK for the USAAF, re-designated R4D-6 for the Navy, and converted by Douglas to R4D-8 (called C-117D since 1962). This Super 3 was operated by US Marines at Iwakuni, Japan after WWII and is at the Marine Corps Station El Toro Command Museum, El Toro, CA. Note the wire antenna and also the fin design, a 'Torii' or Japanese shrine gate. (Photo February 1997)

This C-117D, registered N587MB, has operated scheduled weekday cargo flights to Nassau, Bahamas since 1994, by Dragon Air Leasing from Opa Locka, FL. The engines are Wright Cyclone R-1820s. Note the one-piece windscreen, intake and pitot heads on the nose. The rudder and elevators are not yet painted. (Photo May 1998)

Genavco Air Cargo, Honolulu International Airport, Honolulu, HI, has used two DC-3s and one Super 3 for cargo and charter work, parachute jumping, films and TV programmes. N9796N, an R4D-5-DK later (C-117D), is now used mainly for scheduled parcel services between the Hawaiian islands. The nose intake and pitot heads can be seen as the aircraft taxies. (Photo April 1998)

This R4D-8 (C-117D), registered in the Dominican Republic as HI-545CT, is at Deland, FL awaiting sale. The propellers of the Wright Cyclone R-1820 taken from a Grumman Tracker can be seen, as can the large dorsal fin. The aircraft is tied down as a hurricane precaution. (Photo May 1998)

This R4D-8 (C-117D), N505C, was operated by Sky Charter Cargo at Opa Locka, FL. The Super 3 was wrecked, along with about half-a-dozen DC-3s, by a hurricane in February 1998. As well as the port engine, the fuselage was damaged. Her owner, Charles Riggs, said, 'I will restore her and fly again.' (Photo May 1998)

Owned by Basler Turbo Conversion Inc and found in Tucson, AZ, this R4D-8 (LC-117D), 12441, seen on the left, was named *City of Invercargill*. She was fitted with skis and operated to Antarctica by the US Navy. Based at Christchurch, NZ, where she is now replaced by LC-130s, she flew via Invercargill to Antarctica. (Photo February 1997)

This R4D-8 (C-117D), 12412, owned by Air Power, Lakeport, CA, is in desert storage with Dross Metals Inc., Tucson, AZ. Despite their poor appearance, these aircraft stay in very good condition in the desert and many have a good future. Engines, instruments, fuel tanks and other parts are removed for storage and windows and intakes are protected by covers. Twenty-two Super 3s and one C-47 are stored here. In the foreground are parts of C-133s and in the background DC-6s can be seen. Today, 12412 is the youngest Super 3 in the world. (Photo February 1997)

C-53-DO, registered N23SA, is seen in Polair colours (2nd left), outside the Basler Turbo Conversion hangar at Wittman Airport, Oshkosh, WI. Named *Tri Turbo Three*, and *Spirit of Hope*, Conroy Aircraft Corporation converted it to a Turbo-DC-3. J. M. Conroy Specialized Aircraft Company later converted it to a Turbo 3 with three P & W Canada PT-6 turbo-prop engines. Basler Turbo Conversion bought it from desert storage at Mojave, CA and carried it by road to Wittman, where it is seen stored with other DC-3s. In the factory every part is cleaned and checked. The cockpit is modernised with new instruments and the fuselage is stretched. P & W Canada turbo-prop PT-6 engines are fitted, with new cowlings and nacelles, and Hartzell five-blade metal propellers. Among other changes are reinforced centre section, wings and floor (with cargo winch), new wing-tips and leading edges, metal control surfaces and a wide cargo door for LD3 containers. It will fly in the twenty-first century as a BT-67. (Photo April 1997)

Basler Turbo Conversion rolls out its latest BT-67 from the hangar at Oshkosh, WI. The aircraft, registered as TZ 390 is being ferried to its new owner, the Mali Air Force. Note the emergency fuel dumping pipes on the inboard wing trailing edges. (Photo September 1998)

This BT-67, seen at Missoula, MT, was converted to a turbo prop by Basler Turbo Conversion for the US Forest Service and delivered 18 June 1991. The USFS has used two BT-67s for smoke-jumpers, who jump from the aircraft to fight fires carrying 100–110 pound bags. One USFS staff member joked, 'The BT-67 is excellent. High-powered engine, doesn't lose oil and maintenance is just pat an engine.' Note the safety covers on the rear of the troop door and on the tail wheel to protect the jumpers. (Photo September 1997)

OLD AIRLINERS

This DC-3-277B is seen at American Airlines C. R. Smith Museum, Euless, TX. AA operated from Dallas, TX, in the 1930s. Seeking longer routes, they ordered a DC-2 in sleeper configuration. Douglas converted and the result was two feet six inches wider than a normal DC-2. Berths were later changed to seats and the type was replaced by Convair 240s in the early 1950s. NC21798, flagship *Knoxville* number 98, is painted in 1930s AA colours. The body and interior are restored to original condition. The interior is laid out as seven rows of three abreast, with a kitchen, toilet and baggage space at the rear. Features such as hat racks and air louvers are similar to today's aircraft interiors. The museum is named after the president of AA who opened discussions with Douglas about the DC-3. (Photo March 1997)

Used between December 1937 and September 1952, and logging 56,782 flying hours, this DC-3-201, NC18124, was donated to the National Air & Space Museum of the Smithsonian Institution, Washington, DC in May 1953 and has been displayed since July 1976. Because of her early retirement and one-owner history with Eastern Airlines she has no major modifications and is possibly in the closest original condition of any DC-3 in the world today. She hangs from ceiling-mounted wires, below a Ford Tri-Motor and above a Boeing 247. Note the loop antenna beneath the nose. Eastern operated DC-2s from April 1934 to December 1940 and DC-3s from then until 1953. (Photo October 1997)

This DC-3-277B, NC25673, owned by Continental Airlines Historical Society, is based in Dallas, TX. The is used for air shows, company customer flights and company advertising. The Wright engines on the original American Airlines version were changed by purchaser Trans Texas Airways to P & Ws which are on the aircraft today. Note the one-piece windscreen, the right-hand passenger door, the short engine exhausts and the pitot heads moved to the nose. The cabin air vents are visible on the upper fuselage. The aircraft is seen at Houston, TX, Continental's maintenance base, taxiing for a return flight to Dallas. (Photo March 1997)

Seen in the Delta Airlines DC-3 restoration hangar, Delta's first hangar, where the airline's history began, is DC-3-357, N29PR. The restoration project received three DC-3s, using two for parts to restore the third. Much of the aircraft skin has also been replaced. Delta Airlines Inc operated DC-2s and DC-3s between 1940 and 1963. The fifth window in the picture, abeam the wing trailing edge is the escape hatch. (Photo May 1998)

Western Airlines Inc, Los Angeles, CA, operated DC-3s from 1937 to 1954. They merged with Delta in 1987 and this DC-3A-197E, NC33644, was originally part of their fleet. Now owned by Mike Kimberl, a Delta pilot who flies it in his spare time, it is named *Mary Linda II* after his wife. Mike owns a large property with a private 1900 ft airstrip and finds the DC-3 useful with his wife and fifteen children. The aircraft can be seen starting up for an evening pleasure flight. (Photo April 1997)

Seen in Ozark Air Lines colours, this C-53-DO/R4D-3-DO, N763A is owned by the Prairie Aviation Museum at Bloomington Normal Airport, Bloomington, IL. Ozark, of St Louis, MO, operated DC-3s between 1950 and 1968 when they were replaced by F-27s and FH227Bs. The generator air intake can be seen aft of the cockpit window. The fifth and sixth passenger windows are escape hatches and the aircraft has the passenger door on the left. At the starboard wing root can be seen the high-speed wing fillet. (Photo May 1998)

Now owned by the Museum of Flight, Boeing Field, Seattle, WA, this DC-3-455/C-49K-DO was part of Alaska Airlines' original fleet. They operated DC-3s out of Seattle from 1945 to 1958. One of two DC-3s owned by the museum, this aircraft is seen in front of a Boeing factory building, with both wings off and awaiting restoration. The registration NC was used in the US until December 1948, C standing for 'Commercial'. The designation C-49K was used for DC-3s with side seating for troops. It has Wright engines and fifty-seven were built for airlines. (Photo October 1997)

Rescued from Melbourne's Tullamarine International Airport car park in April 1987, where she had been on static display since December 1979, C-47-DL, VH-AES, was restored to flying condition by August 1988. Owned by Qantas Hawdon Operations and still kept at Tullamarine, she is in the old colours of Trans Australia Airlines, with the lower fuselage polished, natural metal. Named *Hawdon* after the explorer Joseph Hawdon, she can be seen preparing to taxi out for an air show. (Photo November 1996)

This C-47A-20-DK is owned by the 1st Austrian DC-3 Dakota Club and is undergoing partial (non-flying) restoration at Salzburg Airport. She will be displayed in front of the airport terminal and will be used as a club meeting room and café in the near future. She is painted as OE-LBC, *Edelweiss*, in Austrian Airlines colours. Austrian Airlines (Österreichische Luftverkehr AG) operated three DC-3s between 1963 and 1966. Note the panoramic passenger window and the one-piece cockpit windscreen. (Photo July 1998)

Jacked-up on display at Aviodome, Schiphol Centrum, Amsterdam above the forward section of a D.H.C.-2 Beaver, is C-47A-40-DL, G-BVOL, an ex-South African Air Force aircraft, now painted in KLM's 'Flying Dutchman' colour scheme. Notice the extra, small window above and behind the cockpit. The nose is plastic. (Photo July 1998)

Martin's Air Charter, Amsterdam operated DC-3s between 1960 and 1967, replacing them with Convairs. Martin's is the main sponsor for the Dutch Dakota Association, who owns this C-47A-80-DL, PH-DDZ, in Martin's colours. With 80% of the skin renewed it is being perfectly restored. DDA has one DC-2, two DC-3s, two DC-4s and one Stinson V-76. It has a DC-2 restoration project underway, hoping to have a flyable aircraft in ten to fifteen years, if it can raise enough money. In the left foreground can be seen the cockpit instrument panel. Under the nose is a faired direction-finding aerial. (Photo July 1998)

Painted in early Swissair colours as HB-IRN, this C-53-DO is owned by Flughafen München Besucher park and displayed at Munich New Airport near the car park. Swissair used DC-2s from December 1934 to February 1935 and DC-3s from 1937 to 1969. They were replaced by Convairs. The aircraft's elevators are missing, removed for restoration. (Photo July 1998)

MILITARY AIRCRAFT

On loan from the USAF museum and painted in USAAF colours with D-Day invasion stripes, this C-47-DL is displayed at the Pima Air and Space Museum, Tucson, AZ. The second produced by the Long Beach factory, it is the oldest surviving C-47 in the world. The rudder and elevators have been replaced in metal. (Photo February 1997)

Once a World War II hangar for B-17s, this hangar at Forbes
Field, Topeka, KS now houses a collection for the Combat
Air Museum. C-47B-30-DK, N710Z, pictured here in D-Day
colours is in flying condition. (Photo February 1997)

Painted in D-Day stripes, this C-47-13-DK, 43-48932, is at the 82nd Airborne Division Museum, Fort Bragg, NC. Paratroop training towers can be seen in the background. Note the astrodome on the upper fuselage, rearwards of the cockpit. (Photo May 1998)

Displayed at the Aerospace Museum, Cosford, this C-47B-35-DK is preserved as KG374. It is painted in D-Day colours with black and white stripes on wings and rear fuselage. The first passenger windows are different from usual, revealing its role as a VIP transport. The open passenger door is custom-made. Note the double blowers, the wire antenna, the pilot escape hatch and astrodome to the rear of the cockpit roof. (Photo July 1998)

The C-47 Dakota is affectionately known as a 'Dak' in Great Britain. This C-47A-85-DL, 315509 is displayed at the Imperial War Museum, Duxford Airfield, Duxford in D-Day colours. 'W7' is a 37th Squadron code marking. It is displayed with many other aircraft. The engines are Pratt & Whitney fourteen-cylinder radials, R-1830-92 Twin Wasps of 1200 hp, one of the best all-round radial engines ever built. (Photo July 1998)

This DC-3-455/C-49K-DO is one of fifty-seven built. It has Wright Cyclone R-1820-71 1200 hp engines and was used for USAAF trooping flights, hence *General Delivery* on the nose. Owned by the Experimental Aircraft Association Air Adventure Museum and displayed in front of the EAA headquarters building at Wittman Field, Oshkosh, WI, the maintenance and painting of the aircraft has been supported by Basler Turbo Conversion. (Photo April 1997)

This C-53D-DO, N130Q, owned by Folsom's Air Service, Greenville, ME, is the largest float plane in the world. Whilst not original, the aircraft is designated as XC-47C, and as an experimental plane can not be used commercially. Nicknamed *Dumbo* she has Wright Cyclone R-1820 engines and is fitted with two Edo Model 78 floats. These floats can carry 300 US gallons (1136 litres) of fuel. Only five XC-47Cs were built. Note the one-piece windscreens and plastic nose. The main gears and tail gear have been removed and the left passenger door has a built-in stair. (Photo September 1997)

The Berlin Airlift took place between 1948 and 1949. After World War II and the beginning of the 'Cold War', West Berlin was cut-off from the west and relief began in late June 1948. The USAF and RAF brought food, medicine, fuel and more to Berlin's Tempelhof Airport using DC-3s, C-47s, C-54s, Avro Yorks, Short Sunderlands, B-24s and other aircraft. This C-47B-10-DK, 43-49081, named *The Berlin Train*, is displayed at the Berlin Airlift Memorial, Rhein Main Air Base, Frankfurt along with a C-54. The memorial is only open to the public on Sundays. (Photo July 1998)

This C-47B-1-DL, N54610, is at the Vermont Air National Guard Heritage Park, Burlington International Airport, Burlington, VT. It is undergoing restoration by the ANG for display in the near future. The base was used for P-47s and P-51s in the 1940s and is now a base for Vermont ANG F-16s. Note the astrodome and the fifth window escape hatch. (Photo September 1997)

Along with a Sikorsky H-53 Sea Stallion and a Bell 209/AH-1W Super Cobra this R4D-6-DK, 17278, is in a collection store hangar of the US Marine Corps Air Ground Museum, Quantico, VA. The wings have been removed for storage and she awaits restoration for museum display. The hangar is not open to the public. (Photo October 1997)

Painted in New York Air National Guard colours, this C-47B-25-DK, 44-76457, is owned by Gateway National Recreation Area and displayed at Floyd Bennett Field, Brooklyn, NY. The airfield was closed in the 1960s and is now used as a recreation area. The engine cowlings are protected against birds nesting and hail damage can be seen on the fuselage. Note the double blowers, astrodome and de-icing boots on the leading edges. (Photo October 1997)

On loan from the Smithsonian NASM to the US Naval Aviation Museum and kept at the collection store area at Pensacola, FL, this R4D-5-DL, 12418, was the first aircraft to land at the South Pole. Named *Que Sera Sera*, she took part in 'Operation Deep Freeze' on 31 October 1956, following the exploring tradition of Amundsen and Scott. She is converted for the extreme weather, having engine oil cooler intakes removed, skis fitted to all landing gear and, housed in the extended nose, a weather radar. On the underside can be seen the attachment points for Jet Assisted Take-Off bottles. Nineteen JATO bottles were fitted. Note also the wide window aft and the fuel dumping pipework. (Photo March 1997)

Now at the College of Engineering and Technology, Ohio University, Athens, OH, this C-47A-30-DK, N7AP, is in FAA colours. The FAA, based at Oklahoma City, OK, used sixty DC-3s for flight inspection and other work from 1957 to 1961. The aircraft were overhauled, new systems were installed and special modifications made. After the work was completed, fifty-nine DC-3s were declared surplus. The last DC-3, N34, retired in 1997 and will go to Oklahoma City Science Museum for display. N7AP has extra windows behind the cockpit for electronics technicians and has a stair door fitted. The lower beacon can be seen as she taxies out for a weekend air show. (Photo September 1997)

Today, Hurlburt Field, FL is an AC-130 gunship base. AC-130, AC-119 and this AC-47 (on loan from the USAF Museum) are on display, a perfect collection of three gunship types. Painted in Vietnam War camouflage, 43510 has a black-painted underside for night missions. Rescue markings can be seen above two windows. Three 7.62mm mini-guns delivering 18,000 rounds per minute are fitted. The AC-47 was used in 1966, early in the Vietnam War and was later replaced by AC-119s and AC-130s, all operated as 'truck-busters' along the 'Ho Chi Minh Trail'. Variously nicknamed *Puff*, *Puff the Magic Dragon* and *Dragonship*, this aircraft carries *Spooky* as its nose art. (Photo March 1997)

Here at Kelly Air Force Base, San Antonio, TX is displayed the *Electric Goon*, on loan from the USAF Museum. Converted from a C-47B-1-DK and designated EC-47, this aircraft was used for electronic reconnaissance and psychological warfare. It is painted in Vietnam War camouflage with daylight underside and carries many aerials that betray its role. On the mid-upper fuselage beneath the wire antenna is a blade antenna. Just aft of the astrodome mounting (dome removed) is a system X antenna and above and below the wing, just outboard of the gear are two more system X antennae. Note also the double blowers. Control surfaces are now metal. This aircraft is displayed near the base gate. (Photo February 1997)

This C-47B-1-DL, OT-CWG/K-16, is displayed at the Musée Royal de l'Armée, Brussels, Belgium in Belgian Air Force colours. The Belgian Air Force retired its last C-47 in 1976. Note the double blowers, the Ram/Non-Ram dust filter, the astrodome, wire antenna and the rain gutter above the left-hand passenger door. Two fuel caps and a catwalk are at the wing root on each side and the aircraft has four fuel tanks fitted in the centre section. Other classic aircraft seen are, clockwise from left, Douglas A-26B Invader, de Havilland DH.98 Mosquito NF30, Fairey Battle I, Bristol 149 Bolingbroke IVT, Hawker Hurricane IIC, Supermarine 361 Spitfire LF IXC, Fairchild 110 Flying Boxcar (C-119G) and Percival P.66 Pembroke C.51. (Photo July 1998)

Displayed at the Flugwerft Schleissheim-Deutsches Museum, Munich, this C-47B-20-DK, 14+01, is one of the Luftwaffe's last C 47s to operate, being withdrawn from use in 1976. It is painted in camouflage colours with orange stripes and orange wing-tips, cowlings, nose, rudder and elevators. Rescue markings can be seen on the fuselage sides. The engines are fitted with double blowers. Beneath the starboard wing a P & W R-1830 engine is displayed. The upper wings are littered with paper planes thrown by children. (Photo July 1998)

The Flugausstellung L. und P. Junior, at Hermeskeil, near Trier, Germany is a private museum owned by Leo and Peter Junior and has hundreds of aircraft. The C-47A-75-DL here is displayed in its Royal Jordanian Air Force colours, registered 111. The RJAF operated four C-47s between 1967 and 1977, replaced by C-130s. Alongside the C-47 is a Construcciones Aeronauticas (CASA) 2 111D, a Spanish-built Heinkel He-111 H-16. (Photo July 1998)

This Royal Australian Air Force C-47B-20-DK, is preserved as a gate guardian at Gatow Air Force base, Gatow, near Berlin and is known as a Kangaroo C-47 in Germany. The RAAF once operated 124 C-47s and now uses four out of Edinburgh, near Adelaide for cargo work. A65-69 has only 13,366 flying hours. Note the astrodome, double blowers and the air vent aft of the rearmost passenger window. (Photos July 1998)

This C-47B-30-DK, 6023, was used as an R4D-7 navigator trainer and an R4D-6Q electronic countermeasures trainer. It is seen here at Kanoya Base Aviation Museum, Kanoya, Kagoshima prefecture, Japan in its ECM role. Kanoya Base was a 'Kamikaze' base during World War II and afterwards used by the Japanese Marine Self Defence Force as a base for sea and anti-submarine patrols by TBMs, PV-2s and PBYs in the 1950s, S2Fs and P2s in the 1960s and now for P3Cs. Four R4D-6s operated here between 1958 and 1974. Note the Day-Glo orange markings on the aircraft extremities. The fin has been reinforced against typhoons and a cover is missing from a lower ECM aerial. (Photo June 1995)

Shown at the Chinese Air Force Museum, Kangshan base, a cargo field near Kaohsiung, China, this is one of the last six C-47s that were operated by the Chinese. They have now been replaced by C-130s. This C-47B-7-DK, 48806, was used as a VIP transport. The passenger windows are non-standard, the front cabin being for VIP use, the rear for staff. The engines have double blowers. As a typhoon precaution reinforced bands are fitted to control surfaces. Parked before the museum building, in front of the C-47, is another VIP transport, a DC-6B. (Photo June 1996)

Outside the School of Aerospace Medicine, Jakarta, Indonesia is this C-47A-25-DK, PK-GDH, in Indonesian Air Force colours and marked as TNI-AU of the 2nd Squadron. The interior is in original condition, with collapsible trooping-seats. Note the 2nd Squadron insignia of Pegasus flying over a cloud with the number two. The Indonesian Air Force once operated fifty-five C-47s, but now the Air Force has only five. (Photo June 1996)

At the Royal Thai Air Force Museum, Don Muang Air Force Base, near Bangkok is 76517, a C-47B-25-DK used by the RTAF as a VIP transport. It has an executive interior. The RTAF had large C-47 and C-123 fleets with over thirty C-47s. These will be converted to PT-6 Turbo-prop engines by Basler Turbo Conversion, Oshkosh, WI. Note the rain gutter of the left passenger door, the double blowers, the lack of cowl flaps, the astrodome and the many radio antennae. Just behind the C-47 a Beech 18 (C-45F) and a C-123 can be seen. (Photo June 1996)

Seen here at its base field, Base Aérea San Isidro, Santo Domingo, Dominican Republic, is FAD3404, a TC-47B-30-DK, which has been stored for display purposes. Another three C-47s are still operating with Fuerza Aérea Dominicana. The aircraft is painted in FAD's camouflage scheme and has double blowers and an astrodome. Fabric control surfaces have been replaced by metal, as fabric rots in the strong sunlight. (Photo April 1998)

CARGO

In Millardair colour scheme with the title of Alaska Island Air who owns and operates her, this C-47B-35-DK, N32AL, is shown at base in Kotzebue, AL. Alaska Island Air uses her for cargo flights to remote areas of Alaska, carrying mainly salmon and daily necessities. She is well proofed against the hard Alaskan weather and many skin patches can be seen. (Photo July 1997)

Cape Smythe Air Services uses this C-47A-30-DK, N19454, for cargo flights to remote Alaskan areas, carrying cargoes of salmon and daily necessities for remote communities. She flies out of Kotzebue, AL. The fabric rudder fin has been recently renewed and has not yet been repainted. (Photo July 1997)

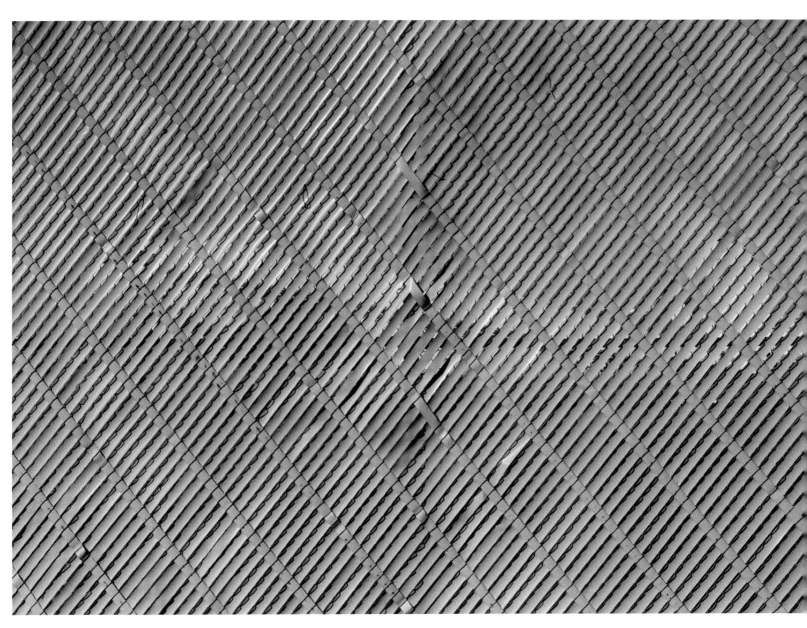

This photograph was taken at Long Beach, CA and is an eyesight test. It is, in fact, a C-47B-45-DK, N403JB, belonging to Catalina Flying Boats and painted white with a blue strip, similar to the classic Air France design. Catalina Flying Boats uses two DC-3s for cargo flights to Santa Catalina Island off the Californian coast. (Photo January 1997)

Restored and used by Air Tejas, this C-47A-20-DK, N941AT, performs cargo operations out of Georgetown, TX. *Vera Lynn II* is seen with full flaps down for landing. Note the unusual double landing lights in each wing. Note also the one-piece windscreen and the patched passenger windows indicating cargo use. (Photo March 1997)

This C-47A-50-DL, N12BA, is owned by Viking Express who used her for cargo flights. Here at Aurora Municipal Airport, Aurora, IL, the cowlings and wings are off for maintenance prior to sale. Both aircraft in this photograph are for sale, which would you buy? (Photo September 1997)

Here, taxiing for take-off is N142JR, a C-47B-25-DK, belonging to Rhoades Aviation. It operates four C-47s out of Colombus, IN, as cargo planes. The other two, N140JR and N139JR (minus engines), can be seen in the background. (Photo September 1997)

Miami Valley Aviation has used six DC-3s for cargo, plus four Beech 18s and others, carrying mainly car parts. One of its DC-3s is leased to a flying doctor group in Nashville, TN. These pictures show N9923S, a C-47B-5-DK, taxiing and tail-up for take off at its base, Middletown Hook Field, Middletown, OH. The number '99' on the fin is the MVA fleet number. (Photo September 1997)

This photograph shows another of Miami Valley Aviation's DC-3s at Middletown, OH. This a C-47A-30-DK, N8187E. The aircraft are kept extremely busy carrying cargo, mainly, but not exclusively, car parts. This shot shows the plastic nose and one-piece windscreens, also the short engine exhausts. In the background is a Beech 18 (C-45). (Photo June 1998)

IFL, operating out of Pontiac, MI, used seven DC-3s for cargo work, mainly carrying car parts, but has now replaced them with Convairs. Two of the seven are seen here. The aircraft in the foreground is a C-47-A-20-DK, N683LS, sold to Flamenco Airways, Culebra, Puerto Rico. The one in the background is a C-47A-45-DL, N303SF, sold to Dodson International Air, Oxford, GA and then to Four Star Aviation, St Thomas, VI. (Photo September 1997)

DKI is a DC-3 trading company, specialising in DC-3 spare parts, maintenance and DC-3 owners' support. This C-47A-DL, N345AB, is seen reflected on the DKI hangar in Redding, PA. (Photo October 1997)

Operated by Dodson International Air out of Covington, GA this C-47B-1-DL, N2805J is seen at Opa Locka, FL. Dodson uses six DC-3s for cargo work. The power of the P & W R-1830 engines with double blowers is useful in the bad weather seen here. Lined up behind N2805J, in a scene reminiscent of D-Day, are Florida Air Cargo's DC-3 N15MA and an unidentified Super 3. (Photo April 1998)

Academy Airlines of Griffin and Thomaston, GA has been operating three DC-3s on cargo flights for nearly thirty years. The airline has DC-3 expertise and also trades in DC-3 spare parts. This C-47A-80-DL, N130D, was leased for a TV programme called 'Animal House' and has retained the colour scheme used for the programme. Painted on the right-hand side, front to rear are a gorilla, a kangaroo, a camel, a giraffe, a panther, a chameleon, a reindeer and a bear with ivy. On the left is a gorilla, a rhinoceros, an alligator, an elephant, an ostrich and a tiger with ivy. The scheme is completed with animal footprints on the tail. This DC-3 is a nocturnal animal, sleeping during the day and coming out at night to freight newspapers between towns. (Photo May 1998)

This DC-3-227A, N143D, is one of the three DC-3s used by Academy Airlines for cargo since 1974. Seen here at take off from Thomaston, GA, her long career seemed over when she crashed into a swamp in Florida in September 1984. She was rescued from the alligator infested waters by winches and wires, and repaired. She is now called *Miss Ali Gater*. (Photo May 1998)

C-47A-DL, N705GB, is one of two DC-3s used for cargo flights to Caribbean islands by Atlantic Air Cargo, operating out of Miami International Airport, FL. Here she is seen taking a cargo of flowers to the Bahamas, taxiing among jets at Miami's busy airport. (Photo May 1998)

Based at Jackson, MS this C-47-DL, N8061A, flown by Jim Hankins Air Service is seen at Destin, FL. Jim Hankins operates this DC-3 for cargo. The aircraft is powered by P & W R-1830-90D engines and painted in FAA colour scheme with blue stripes instead of red. (Photo March 1997)

Air North Charter & Training owned and operated C-47A-5-DK, CF-OVW out of Whitehorse, YK, Canada. Here, she is beautifully painted with a yellow roof, green stripes, natural metal and light-grey fuselage underside. Air North DC 3s have names with Northern Canadian associations. CF-OVW was named *Yukon Sourdough*. The aircraft now belongs to EAA at Oshkosh, WI. (Photo July 1997)

Parked at Whitehorse, with engines protected by wood panels, is C-47A-20-DK, C-FIMA, one of Air North's four DC-3s. The DC-3s are used for cargo and passenger flights to Alaska and sometimes for smoke-jumpers fighting forest fires. The DC-3s are all named: C-FIMA *Yukon Musher* (dog sled), CF-CUG *Lady Lou* (a show dancer), CF-OVW *Yukon Sourdough* (a Yukon River gold-digger) and CF-GHL *Vadzaih Naataii* (Wandering Caribou). (Photo July 1997)

Trans Fair, based at Longue-Pointe-de-Mingan, QC, uses two DC-3s for government contract cargo flights to remote areas in the winter season. They carry food, fuel, indeed everything people need to survive the snowy winters of Northern Canada. The airline believes the DC-3s, fitted with skis, are best for this big-cargo ski-plane work. Note the double blowers, astrodome, two upper beacons and conspicuous orange wing tips and tail. Parked, the engines are covered against the cold weather. (Photo June 1997)

Pictured here is the second of Trans Fair's DC-3s used for cargo flights in northern Canada. C-47A-30-DK, C-FDTT, is hangared at Longue-Pointe-de-Mingan, QC. Clearly seen on the starboard wing tip are the green navigation light and static discharge wick. Behind the cockpit can be seen the extra windows installed when the aircraft was used by the FAA. The engine is covered and the aircraft has an orange fuselage-band for visibility in winter. (Photo June 1997)

Swiftair, of Manila, Philippines has operated three DC-3s for cargo and passengers. Here at the west maintenance area of Manila Domestic Airport is RP-C147, a C-47B-1-DL, its engines covered with blue tarpaulins. Still in Manila are one Super 3 and fourteen DC-3s, four of the DC-3s being in storage. They are used for charter flights carrying mainly foodstuffs – rice, fish, chicken and so on. They are occasionally used for carrying parts and sometimes for passengers, scenic flights and filming. Many DC-3s have been destroyed in the Philippines, by crashes and by strong summer-season typhoons. (Photo July 1996)

Pictured here at Manila Domestic Airport's west maintenance area are three DC-3s, C-47A-30-DKs, of Avia Filipinas (FIL). In silver is RP-1353, in white is RP-1354 and the wing tip in military colour belongs to RP-1352. These three DC-3s were used for an Australian film, 'Anchor'. FIL has used four DC-3s for cargo, and for charter pleasure flights and filming. (Photo July 1996)

Without engines, her rudder and elevators fabric-less skeletons, RP-C74, a C-47A-30-DK sits at Manila Domestic Airport's west maintenance area. Owned by Mabuhay Airways Philippines, it is not known whether she will be restored or used for spare parts. In the background is RP-C473, a Super 3. (Photo July 1996)

Seen at Seletar Airport, Singapore, this C-47A-80-DL, is owned by Airfast Indonesia. The aircraft, based at Jalankayu, Singapore, is their last DC-3 in service. The company is a large, Indonesian, helicopter concern. PK-OAZ is used for passenger and cargo services and is fitted with twenty-one seats. Note the plastic nose, one-piece windscreens and the lack of engine cowl flaps, unnecessary in the tropics. (Photo June 1996)

Here at Las Americas International Airport cargo area in Santo Domingo, Dominican Republic, is this C-47-DL, HI-465 belonging to Aerolincas Argo. The aircraft, with patched first and seventh windows, is being broken up for parts and scrap. In the background is another Argo aircraft, a Lockheed L-749A Constellation, HI-393. The Dominican Republic is a graveyard for old aircraft. Because of US Government restrictions on illegal carriers, many flights from the Dominican Republic to Miami have ceased and the aircraft are waiting to be broken up. Here, at Las Americas are one Lockheed L-749 Constellation, two L-1098 Super Constellations, three Curtiss C-46 Commandos, one DC-4, two DC-6s, one DC-7, one DC-3 and two Convairs. (Photo April 1998)

SPECIAL OPERATIONS

Tropical South Florida, with its high humidity and alligator swamps, has large numbers of mosquitoes which breed at the end of the rainy season. Lee County Mosquito uses ten DC-3s (seven flying, three for parts) and many Bell 205 UH-1H Iroquois for mosquito spraying under government contracts. The front and rear DC-3s are smokers, which emit a mixture of diesel and anti-mosquito chemicals from their exhausts: the middle two are sprayers, with a high-pressure spray bar under each wing. Note the rear-view mirror mounted by the left cockpit side window. (Photo May 1998)

Taxiing for an engine test run at Houma-Terrebonnc Airport, Bourg, LA, is N64766, a C-47B-20-DK, operated by EASI Mosquito Control. The glider tow hook mounting is patched, as are the two astrodome mountings, telling of a previous role as a navigation trainer. Spray bars under the wings can be seen. These bars are supplied with chemicals from a large tank in the aircraft cabin and the spray is for either mosquito control or for dispersing oil pollution. EASI uses four DC-3s for this spraying work. (Photo March 1997)

This DC-3A-269C, N496, minus engines, tyres flat, flaps down and covered with moss is being broken for parts by Environmental Aviation Services Inc (EASI) at Houma-Terrebonne Airport, Bourg, LA. In the background can be seen EASI's DC-4 sprayer on a test flight. EASI conducts spraying flights for mosquito control and for spraying dispersants on oil spills. (Photo March 1997)

This aircraft, an R4D-1-DL, N737H, is operated by Texas Instruments out of Dallas, TX. Seen here starting engines at Pottsboro, TX, it is a flying test-bed for the company. It is fitted with many special instruments, TV monitors, recorders, a geographic camera, numerous antennae and a gasoline generator for producing electric power. Note the short exhaust pipes smoking at start-up and the undercarriage half-doors, part of the high-speed kit. On the nose is an air intake and a mounted TV camera. (Photo March 1997)

N4991E, a C-47A-1-DK is owned by William C. Dause Jr and operates from Lodi, CA near San Francisco. Bill Dause uses it for parachute jumping, taking up to thirty jumpers at one time. It is fitted with Pratt & Whitney R-2000 engines with spinners and oil-coolers from a DC-4. The cabin interior has been covered with stickers by parachute jumpers. Note the rear-view mirror on the cockpit side. (Photo April 1997)

Lodi, CA is a famous sky-diving base. Today there are two DC-3s at Lodi Airport. This one, silhouetted against the sunset sky is a C-53D-DO, N45366, owned by DC-3 Flights. It has Wright Cyclone R-1820 engines. (Photo April 1997)

Previously owned by Green County Skydiver, Xenia, OH, but now privately owned this C-53D-DO, N66W was used for parachute jumping. She was kept on a small farm-airstrip amid corn and the aircraft could take forty-three sky-divers and two pilots. (Photo October 1997)

N87745, a DC-3-454 is owned by Zack B. Hinton Jr, Locust Grove, GA. Fitted with Wright Cyclone R-1820 engines and named *Southern Cross*, this DC-3 is used for private pleasure flights. (Photo May 1998)

Pictured here at the first International Air Show in Jakarta, Indonesia at Soekarno-Hatta International Airport, is AF-4776, a C-47A-25-DK. It is owned by Satuan Udara FASI (Flying Association of the Indonesian Services dba), a non-commercial state association conducting mainly flights carrying member parachutists. They operate five DC-3s with one stored. The aircraft is painted as a flying man in traditional Indonesian clothes. The nose is painted with a mouth and nose, the cockpit windows are dark-glasses, arms are painted on the wings and feet on the tail. The mark on the rudder is the FASI emblem. Also seen are: clockwise from left, a Lockheed P3C Orion, a McDonnell Douglas KC-10 Extender, General Dynamics F-16s, an Airbus A340, an Antonov An-124 and a Boeing 777 on a round-the-world sales promotion. In the foreground is a North American NA88 Texan (T-6). (Photo June 1996)

A famous regular at air shows and sometimes used for parachute jumping and filming, N151ZE, an R4D-6-DK, is owned by the Confederate Air Force and is part of their Dallas-Fort Worth Wing. Sporting 'Ready 4 Duty' nose art, it is based at Lancaster, TX and is seen here with cowlings removed for engine maintenance prior to a weekend air show. CAF has another two flying DC-3s at Bloomingdale, IL (Great Lakes Wing) one stored at Brownsville, TX (Rio Grande Valley Wing) and another displayed at Mesa, AZ (Arizona Wing). Note the wire antenna, the astrodome, one-piece window, original WWII GFE antenna under the cockpit window, loop antenna under the nose and the faired DF aerial. The portable extinguisher is needed during engine start. Taxiing in from a test flight is the CAF's F4U Corsair. (Photo May 1997)

The Yankee Air Museum, Belleville, MI has many war-birds in flying condition. This photograph was taken at their open house air show. This C-47B-30-DK, N8704, is seen painted in its old Air Force colours as 476716. The astrodome, a characteristic of the C-47, wire antennae and double blowers can be seen clearly. (Photo September 1998)

One of a number of war planes in flying condition owned by the Mid-Atlantic Air Museum, Reading, PA, this R4D-6-DK, N229GB is seen at its base, Reading Regional Airport. Good restoration has returned this plane to its original R4D condition. Note the stair door and the fixed cargo door. Underneath is a GFE antenna and, forward, two direction-finding antennae and a loop antenna can be seen. There are even curtains on the windows. (Photo October 1997)

The Canadian Warplane Heritage Museum has many flying warplanes. It owns this DC-3-201B, C-GDAK, which has the distinction of having the second highest flying hours of a DC-3 in the world, 81,243 hours at July 1997. Seen at its base, Hamilton Airport, ON, it is painted in green and brown camouflage, and is named *Canucks Unlimited*. It has 'Burma Star' on the nose. Note the nose air intake and the astrodome. The engines are Wright Cyclone R-1820-G102As with short exhaust pipes. (Photo June 1997)

This C-47A-60-DL, ZA-947, is flown by the RAF Battle of Britain Memorial Flight from RAF Coningsby, Lincolnshire, for air shows and parachute drops. She is named *Portpatrick Princess* and at July 1998 had amounted 13,727 flying hours. She is seen making a three-point landing at the 1998 Royal International Air Tattoo at Fairford, England, which also commemorated the 50th anniversary of the Berlin Airlift. (Photo July 1998)

PLEASURE FLIGHTS

Dakota National Air owns seven DC-3s, five operating, two in storage. Used for charter work, scenic flights, private flights and air shows they are based at Bankstown Airport, near Sydney, NSW. The airborne picture shows C-47A-1-DK,

VH-SBL, landing at Bankstown with landing lights on and flaps full down at 45° after a scenic flight over Sydney Harbour. She has thirty-two seats for these flights. (Photo September 1996)

Number '07' of Dakota National Air's fleet of seven DC-3s, VH-BPN is a C-47-30-DK. Here she is parked at Bankstown Airport, NSW, behind '05', VH-PWN which came via the Papua New Guinea Air Force. The opened battery boxes and ground-electric plug door can be seen. (Photo September 1996)

Shortstop Jet Charter of Essendon, Vic, in Australia has restored this C-47B-30-DK, VH-OVM to flying condition and uses her for scenic and charter flights out of Essendon Airport. Named *Arthur H. Schutt*, she bears crew names on the front door and a 'Douglas – First Around the World' emblem. Pictured here after a dinner-flight over Melbourne's Port Phillip Bay she is fitted with twenty-eight seats and powered by Pratt & Whitney R-1830-90C Twin Wasps (1200 hp each) with double blowers. Note the air-stairs and the extra window on the cargo door. (Photo September 1996)

John L. Hardy, owner of Air North Regional, Darwin, NT, has used this C-47A-30-DL, VH-MMA for nearly twenty years. She is fitted with thirty seats and is seen here on the red earth of the airport apron at Bathurst Island, Nguiu, NT. Unable to return to Darwin because of engine trouble, she is waiting for a spare engine. Note the few benches by the airport fence; this is the airport terminal. (Photo October 1996)

ZK-AMS, a C-47A-20-DL, is owned by Pionair Adventures and based at Christchurch, New Zealand. She is named *Spirit of Queenstown* and fitted with twenty-eight seats for scenic and charter flights. She is seen touching down at Queenstown on a ski-tour charter flight. (Photo August 1996)

This classic aircraft, a C-47B-30-DK, ZK-AWP, is seen in the beautiful, modern colours of Classic Air (1994–96) parked at Ardmore Aerodrome, Papakura, near Auckland, NZ. Classic Air operated her with twenty-eight seats on pleasure flights from Wellington, but have now ceased operations. (Photo August 1996)

Era Classic Airlines has two DC-3s that it uses for scenic flights from Anchorage, AL. N1944H is one of them, a C-47B-50-DK equipped with a panoramic window for good viewing on these flights. Note the lights on the engine nacelle, used for checking the upper wing surfaces for ice. She is fitted with one-piece windscreens and a plastic nose cone. (Photo July 1997)

South Coast Airways Ltd, Bournemouth use this C-47A-35-DL, G-DAKK, for scenic flights every weekend. She is fitted with thirty-two seats. Note the beacon moved to the top of the fin and the astrodome on the main cabin roof. (Photo July 1998)

This DC-3 was fitted with thirty seats, and was used by Champlain Enterprises of Plattsburgh, NY for passenger flights. It has now been sold and is going to a new owner in Florida. DC-3-277B, N922CA (2204) is named *Priscilla*. Note the cockpit roof escape hatch, the one-piece windscreen with de-icer tube and the modified position of the pitot tube. (Photo September 1997)

Southwest Aero Parts, San Antonio, TX trades in DC-3s and also sells DC-3 spare parts. XA-REP, a C-47-DL, is being changed from a passenger door to a cargo door version, prior to sale. She was previously used for passenger work in Mexico. Modifications are underway here, with cargo door parts on the ground by the left passenger door. The aircraft is fitted with panoramic windows and the propellers have been removed for maintenance. (Photo February 1997)

N14RD is the only C-41A built and was used as the flagship for General Hap Arnold in WW II. She was owned by Rowan Aviation of Houston, TX, an oil-platform company, and used for their company customers. The aircraft is seen here hangared in very good condition alongside a classic Packard automobile. Note the left-hand passenger door with air-stairs and the cargo door. The undercarriage doors are open and the short engine exhausts and large air-scoops can be seen. (Photo March 1997)

Basler Turbo Conversion had this C-53-DO, N147M, up-rated to P & W R-2000s, with streamlined nacelles and propeller spinners. Wide windows and new undercarriage doors are also fitted. Seen at the Basler base of Wittman Airport, Oshkosh, WI, she was painted in the present colour scheme and named *Billion Dollar One* for the film 'Richie Rich'. The air-conditioned interior with indirect lighting is in executive style for VIP passengers, who also have their own repeater instruments in the cabin. Note the one-piece windscreens and the pitot tube above the nose art. The aircraft is now privately owned. (Photo April 1997)

Once a VIP transport with an executive cabin, this sad-looking aircraft, covered in moss, is N100M, a C-47A-80-DL. She is pictured at Oakland International Airport, Oakland, CA and is used by the Oakland Airport Fire Services for fire training. The hi-speed kit wing fillets are gone as is almost every removable part. Firemen need courage to train inside the fuselage, which is full of birds' nests, cobwebs and beehives, where they can be subject to surprise attacks from the occupants. (Photo April 1997)

DISPLAY

Mounted on pylons and displayed at Oklahoma State Fairground's Exhibition since 1977 is this C-47A-15-DK, 892953. She is seen here behind a Boeing B-47E Stratojet and alongside an Aero Commander L-3805. (Photo April 1997)

A disco and pub owned by Graham Brothers Entertainment in San Antonio, TX is the last resting place of the nose and propellers of this unknown C-47. She carries the name *Mary Lou* and overlooks the dance floor. (Photo March 1997)

This DC-3A-228C was restored to provide an advertising sign for the Weeks Air Museum 'Fantasy of Flight' at Lakeland, FL and is displayed at the end of a grass strip by a motorway. Engines and propellers are missing. (Photo May 1998)

Yukon's Aviation Heritage has this C-47-DL, CF-CPY, at Whitehorse Airport gate, Whitehorse, YK. Mounted at exactly the centre of gravity, on a pole with low-friction bearings, she is the largest weather-vane in the world. She is painted in Canadian Pacific Airlines colours as she was when in service with them. CP operated DC-3s from 1945 to 1969 and their last DC-3 was sold in 1974. (Photo July 1997)

The aviation display hangar of Reynolds Alberta Museum is the home of C-FIAE, a C-47-DL. The picture shows her beautifully polished, natural metal skin. Also shown are the air intake at top left and, mid left, the exhaust of the gasoline generator, needed for cabin heating in the freezing Canadian environment. (Photo July 1997)

From the foreground backwards in this photograph are a Bristol 149 Bolingbroke IVT, a Lockheed 18 Lodestar, a North American NA-108 Mitchell (B-25J) and C-FJWP, a C-47-DL. These aircraft are stored in the stockyards of Reynolds Aviation Museum, Wetaskiwin, AB. In 1919, Ted Reynolds built a monoplane that became the first of a large collection. His son, Stan Reynolds, took over the collection and added to it. Consisting of about a hundred aircraft, many classic cars, tractors, trucks, steamrollers, farm tools and army tanks, it is enormous. (Photo July 1997)

This DC-3-454/C-49J, C-FTDJ, seen at the National Aviation Museum, Rockcliffe Airport, Ottawa, ON, was converted from its airline role into an executive aircraft for VIPs by the Canadair Company. It has fourteen seats and is equipped with couch, tables and a kitchenette. (Photo June 1997)

Werner Kroll, an engineer-mechanic of Samford, Qld, Australia took a C-47A-25-DK, W-12, and hand-built this camper van on a 1939, K-5 International truck chassis from its fuselage. The kangaroo/aircraft silhouette emblem on the side is his own design and the licence plate, VH-DAK is for 'VH', the Australian civil aircraft register and 'DAK' for Dakota. It still sports its astrodome. (Photo October 1996)

In the main street of Taupo, New Zealand, between the Aeroplane Car Company and McDonald's, is ZK-CAW, a C-47A-65-DL. The engines are removed and the roof escape hatch has been converted into the exhaust for an air-conditioning fan. McDonald's customers can eat and drink inside the DC-3 and it is sometimes used for birthday parties. Under the wings is a children's playground. (Photo July 1996)

Rangitikei River Adventure of Mangaweka, New Zealand runs a BP petrol station, organises rafting, jet-boats and bungy jumping, and operates this C-47B-45-DK, ZK-AOK, as a DC-3 café. Painted in the colours of Fieldair, who originally restored the aircraft, this DC-3 was used as a crop-duster. Fieldair Freight operated eleven DC-3s which were replaced by Fletcher FU-34-950Ms. The fixed landing-lights are incorporated into a painted face on the nose. The cabin is equipped as a café, with the rear section used as a kitchen, the radio section as refrigerator space and the remainder as a seating area with about sixteen or eighteen seats. She is named *Weka* after a flightless New Zealand bird. The town name, Mangaweka, means 'Weka's mountain' in Maori. (Photo August 1996)

Separated into large sections, KG437, a C-47A-10-DK, has ended its life as Dakota's American Bistro in Fleet, to the west of London. The fuselage has been cut in two lengthways and a bar fitted between the halves. The nose section with its complete cockpit is placed before the bar to greet visitors as they enter. At the rear is the tail plane and fin, and scattered around the restaurant tables which surround the fuselage are parts from the DC-3 – its tail gear, main gear and engine among others. Over the bar the large, circulating fan is one of its propellers, complete with spinner, and around the walls are some of its instruments. (Photo July 1997)

Mignet 'Flying Flea'

A very early example from the Douglas production line, this DC-3A-197, EI-AYO is owned by the Science Museum and kept at their collection storage hangar at Wroughton, near Swindon in England. Painted white with yellow stripes, it has one-piece windscreens, a plastic nose and undercarriage half doors as hi-speed kit. It stands behind a Bede BD-5B. Special permission is needed to tour the hangar. (Photo July 1998)

The Luchtvaart Hobby Shop near Schiphol Airport, Schiphol, Amsterdam is one of the largest shops selling aircraft goods in the world. It sells books, models, CDs, computer software, pilot aids, pins and more. Behind the computer screen, which is displaying a DC-3 simulation program, is the nose from 42-24211, a C-47A-25-DK. (Photo July 1998)

Deutsche Lufthansa AG used DC-2s between 1938 and 1941 and DC-3s between 1936 and 1960, and this C-47A-30-DK is seen in their colours and as D-CADE, a mark not actually ever registered for this aircraft. It is displayed at the Auto und Technik Museum, Sinsheim, near Heidelberg, Germany.

Visitors to this museum will be amazed at the 'aircraft forest', the large number of aircraft mounted on poles looking like strange trees. Among the numerous aircraft are a Ju52, Il-14, Viscount, many jets and this DC-3. (Photo July 1998)

This C-53-DO, F-BFGX, is in the Air France colour scheme with Air Inter title and is displayed beside a café at the Technikmuseum Speyer, Speyer, Germany. Air Inter, based at Paris Orly, used this DC-3 in 1961, leased from TAI, but soon replaced it. The undercarriage doors show it is fitted with a hi-speed kit. Note the extra windows behind the cockpit. Just visible in the background is a Nord N2501 Noratlas. (Photo July 1998)